The Business of
LEADLIGHTING

The Business of LEADLIGHTING

Will Fraser

Kangaroo Press

Acknowledgments

The author acknowledges with gratitude the advice
and assistance he has received from many sources in
the compilation of this book.

First published in 1995 by Kangaroo Press Pty Ltd
3 Whitehall Road Kenthurst NSW 2156 Australia
PO Box 6125 Dural Delivery Centre NSW 2158 Australia
Typeset by G.T. Setters Pty Limited
Printed in Hong Kong through Colorcraft Ltd

ISBN 0 86417 587 6

CONTENTS

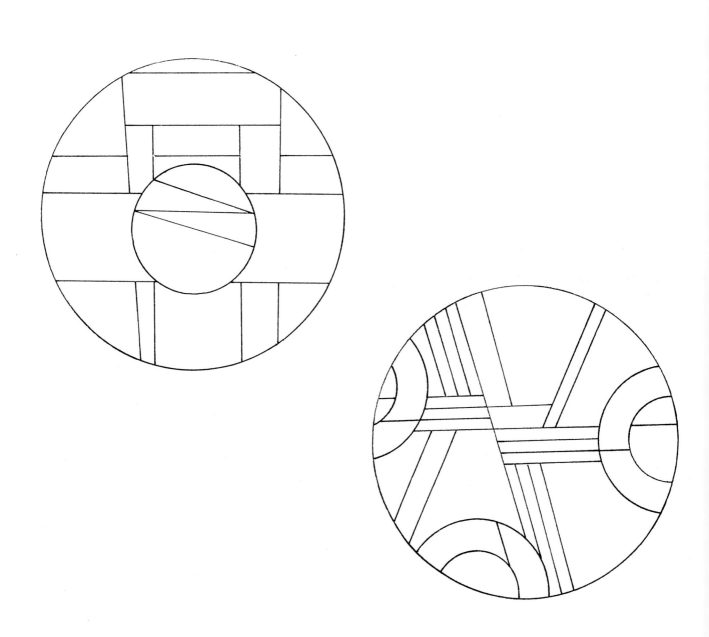

FOREWORD

This book has been written as a guide for those wishing to broaden their leadlight experience by working in all aspects of the craft in the marketplace.

It is also hoped that its contents may serve as a catalyst for self-motivated young people looking for a creative career path.

Information contained in *The Business of Leadlighting* comes from the author's sixteen years' experience designing and making both commercial and art leadlights in New South Wales (Manly, Birchgrove, Mount Victoria, Bathurst), Victoria (Bacchus Marsh, Daylesford, Castlemaine) and also in the United Kingdom (Cornwall).

My sincere thanks to all those people and friends who have supported and encouraged me in the preparation of this book. In particular I thank Tony Stafrace of The Melbourne Glass Centre, and Geoff Butler of Mr. Leadlights, Ballarat, Victoria, for his kind permission to take the black and white shop/studio photographs used in this book.

A professional design and consultant leadlight service is available from:

Will Fraser Leadlights
83 Duke Street
Castlemaine Victoria 3450
Australia

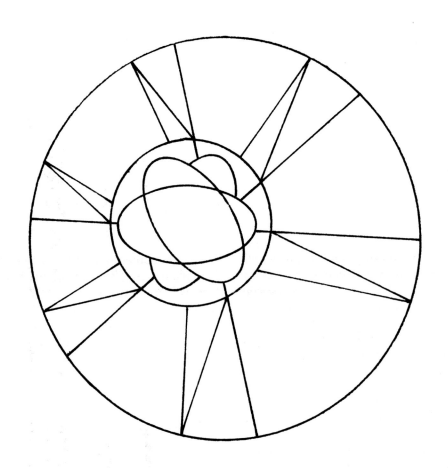

1 GETTING STARTED

Most people start out in the leadlight business making panels for friends and relatives. This is a natural process, for as soon as your immediate circle of friends and relatives learn that you are making leadlights they will contact you with work. A situation such as this has its pluses, but it also has its drawbacks. On the positive side you will get leadlight work that you normally wouldn't be getting and friends and relatives are usually a little easier to please than 'genuine' customers.

The negative side of obtaining this sort of work is that *because* you are working for friends and relatives you will be expected to give them all a special deal! Usually this means labouring over some fantastically complex panel and then being expected to charge next to nothing for your efforts.

By all means work for friends and relatives *but do always* rationalise your projects. Set yourself a *minimum* square metre leadlight charge early on and stick to it! Ring around a few professional leadlighters to find out what their minimum square metre charges are and modify your own minimum charge according to your expertise and work experience.

It is important to set your work habits early as how you start out in business will have a considerable bearing on your professional working life later on.

If you can survive the 'trial by friends and relatives' and come out of that learning time satisfied that your work and rate of pay were fair and reasonable according to the jobs you completed, then you should be ready for the commercial marketplace.

Once you have decided to launch into a leadlight business as a career there are a few general business aspects to consider.

Willingness to work hard

This is the cornerstone of any small business and it is particularly true of leadlighting. You have to be prepared to work hard consistently and often at odd hours in order to get a job completed on time.

Personal flexibility is something you will also need to develop, being able to change your timetable at short notice if and when the need arises.

Setting goals

Personal and financial goals are essential in starting out in your leadlight business so that you have a clear vision of what you are working towards. It is normal for goals to change from time to time—as you progress in your venture so some of your goals will alter.

But you must never lose sight of the goals originally set down, as these are the beacons of success towards which you should be steering your business.

There are two important steps in this forward planning:
1. Visualising your future in terms of three parts—work, home and social life. By dividing your life in this way you will prevent confusion and later conflict.
2. Asking yourself, 'What exactly do I want to accomplish with my business?'

Some of the positive attributes needed for anyone working for themselves in the field of leadlighting include:
- Self-discipline, motivation and creativity.

- Versatility.
- Training and experience.
- Knowledge of the profession.
- An ability to motivate and work with people.
- A willingness and ability to learn new skills, and acquire new knowledge.
- Family support.
- Sufficient capital to finance the business venture.
- An ability to work hard, sometimes under stress.

The business plan

If you have to borrow money from a bank or lending institution to get your business started you will need a business plan to present to them.

Even if you don't have to borrow money to start out it is still an excellent idea to prepare a business plan so that you know precisely what you are going to do.

A business plan must start with a clear picture of what you see and want to achieve in your leadlight business—without concrete objectives you won't be able to proceed.

Your business plan should not be a cumbersome, wordy document full of boring details. Rather it should be short and to the point and consist of coordinated, carefully considered decisions about how your proposed business can best be managed to produce the greatest gains.

In preparing such a plan you should remember to focus on your aims and keep to the point.

The main benefits of preparing such a plan are:
- It at once communicates your business ideas to others such as bankers, financiers and associates.
- As a written plan it acts as a sound foundation for any future planning or expansion.
- It encourages you to make a personal commitment towards achieving the goals set down in the plan.
- It makes you look objectively at what you plan to do, immediately and also for the long term.
- It is a constant reference point against which you can compare what you are trying to achieve and how you are planning to go about it.

The following points should be kept in mind when preparing your business plan:
- Keep the plan as short (and to the point) as possible.
- Plan for 12 months initially.
- Discuss your plan with trusted friends and advisers for valuable feedback.
- It must be realistic, and something you can stick to.

A business plan should contain:
- Your goals and objectives.
- A description of your planned business and the key factors necessary for its success.
- A market analysis of your planned venture incorporating strengths/weaknesses/opportunities/threats.
- Marketing and promotion of your business.
- All financial details (cost of getting business started, source of funding, etc.)
- Time management (when the business will commence, how your time will be spent, breakdown of time, etc.).
- Action planning (what is planned to be done, when, etc.).

Ideally your business plan should contain all the basic facts necessary for a complete stranger to immediately comprehend your proposed leadlight enterprise.

Permissions

If you plan to take out a business name for your leadlight venture you will need to register it with the appropriate government authority.

Similarly, if you plan to start your business off working from home you will need to apply for permission to do so from your local government authority (Council). This also applies to the erection of any business advertising signs at your home in connection with the business conducted there.

2 GAINING CREDIBILITY

Leadlighting is a service. Your customers will only use your special talents if they *(a)* know where you are and, *(b)* are confident that you can offer an efficient and professional service. Gaining workplace acceptance and credibility in both these areas is vital in getting your business to flourish. Letting customers know where you are (be it working from home or from a shop/studio) has to be your first priority when starting out.

Business cards

Business cards should be printed immediately and distributed to all relevant shops/businesses in your immediate vicinity, e.g. glaziers, hardware shops, craft outlets, antique shops, galleries, interior decorators.

Deliver these in person and make yourself known to the proprietors. Spend some time and thought on designing your business card; the card will be an 'advance ambassador' to would-be customers.

It must be both visually artistic, as befits your occupation, and to the point, featuring a logo or design which can from then on be associated with your business, your business name, a brief description of what services you offer (e.g. original creative leadlights, repairs) and your contact telephone number in large type.

Make sure your card is a distinctive colour and looks tasteful as well as dynamic.

Advertising

The second important thing you should do to become known is to advertise.

Most areas have a local paper and some also have a larger regional newspaper which incorporates their municipality. Advertise in both papers to begin with, perhaps giving more emphasis to your local paper by placing a slightly larger advertisement in that publication.

Advertising is expensive so a carefully calculated

programme should be worked out beforehand. Most newspapers will have a rate card (list of advertising prices) which will help you work out costs.

A medium-sized display advertisement is sufficient for most. You should supply the paper with an attractive line drawing, probably of a leadlight design, which can be incorporated into the typeset advertisement.

Whatever logo appears on your business card should always appear in any display advertising you run, thus building on your business identification.

When you start off your business the display ads could perhaps be run every week in your local paper and every fortnight in your regional paper. Later on you could cut this back to once every two weeks in the local paper and once a month in the regional publication.

Regular advertising *is* important. It lets people know that you are in the marketplace and that you are a legitimate business enterprise.

Classified advertising is another way (and cheaper!) of keeping your name and services before the public. Classified advertising is usually only a good idea *after* the more prominent display advertisements have helped establish you in the marketplace.

Free publicity

As soon as you start advertising in your local papers contact their editors and suggest they do a story on you and your work.

A photograph of yourself, perhaps working on a leadlight job, to accompany such a story is always a good idea as it helps to get you known personally.

Make sure you supply sufficient background and professional details to the newspaper reporter to establish your credibility with anyone reading the published story.

Teaching

Introduce yourself (leaving a few business cards) to your local Adult Education or Learning Centre and offer your services as a tutor in leadlighting. This is an excellent way of spreading the word about you and your business which at the same time will provide additional regular income from teaching. Also, by becoming a leadlight tutor you can earn useful extra money by providing and selling glass, lead and tools to those students who enrol in your classes.

If your local Education Centre already has a leadlight course (and tutor), why not run your own classes, either

from home or from your shop/studio? Providing you have sufficient space to comfortably accommodate six to eight students you can successfully run private classes. The advantage of conducting private classes is that you can keep them running without school terms or holiday breaks interrupting the flow.

The more students you teach the better known you and your work will become and you are also bound to pick up commission work from some of your pupils along the way.

Fairs, markets, exhibitions

A further way of increasing your marketplace credibility is to participate in, and be seen at, local markets and fairs and special exhibitions such as Home Shows. Charges for stalls at such events are usually quite reasonable and while you are there you can be working on a current job.

Public exposure at such events is high and you are bound to pick up extra work as a result.

Always remember to market yourself well at these events, having a good supply of business cards available to hand out and a presentation album or book handy, full of photographs of past work and commissions to show to interested members of the public.

These events also present a good opportunity to promote your own leadlight classes.

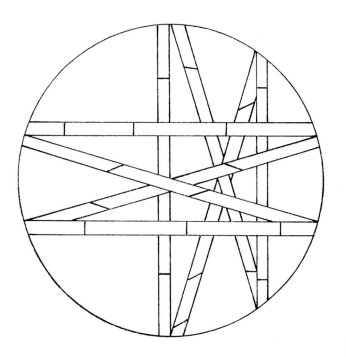

Guest speaking

Another way of increasing your marketplace profile is to contact your local Service Club (Apex, Lions, etc.) and see if you can interest them in having you come along one night as a guest speaker on leadlighting.

This is not as daunting as it might first appear, as you can arm yourself with a slide projector and a swag of slides, showing perhaps a number of internationally famous leadlights and a few of your own works as well. A general potted history of the craft and its current resurgence around the world can be drafted beforehand and read over the slide presentation.

Such personal appearances will add to your public exposure while at the same time putting you in contact with your local business community.

Continuing publicity

Whenever you have special or unusual leadlight commissions to do (e.g. replacing old leadlights in your local church, making a special leadlight for your local hospital or school) contact your local or regional newspaper and suggest they do a photo-story on the work.

In this way you achieve continuity of exposure to the public and further enhance your workplace credibility.

Vehicle identification

No matter what sort of vehicle you choose to use in your business (most leadlighters seem to prefer vans of one type or another), it should have business signs on both sides. These can be either signwritten or, if you are on a tight budget, made-to-order stick-on signs which can be had from most sign suppliers. Remember to include your business logo.

Signed vehicles are a great way of getting your name and telephone number known to the general public as you get about in your day-to-day work activities.

3 THE STUDIO – HOME OR SHOP?

Working from home

Most leadlighters start out working from home, perhaps in a space in the garage or in a spare room somewhere in the house. All too soon you will find that working on the kitchen table, between meals, is not the way to go!

The nature of leadlighting, with its tiny glass fragments and the ever-present lead came, means that it has to be carried out in an area which can be sealed off from children and other family members—and pets. A separate

room is the best option. This way work can be left undisturbed until you have sufficient time to come back to it and potentially dangerous items such as glass, lead and cutting tools are not available to those inexperienced in their use and handling.

Working from home has many advantages:
- No travelling time.
- Low overheads.
- Convenience.
- Tax deductability on the area used for your work as a cottage industry.

But, as with most things, working from home also has its disadvantages. Some of these are:
- The strict discipline required to separate home duties from your professional activities.
- A low public profile.
- The amateur status bestowed on you by the general public, which still equates business and professions with commercial shopfront operations.

Some people who work from home gradually upgrade their working environment, perhaps in time moving out of their garage or spare room into a purpose-built studio erected in the grounds of their home. This can work well if your local Council or Government authority agrees to your studio plans.

Various local Councils have different by-law regulations regarding cottage industries and although it may be all right to work at leadlighting in a spare room of your house, putting up a separate business studio in your garden may not suit your particular Council. Even to start off working from a spare room in your house

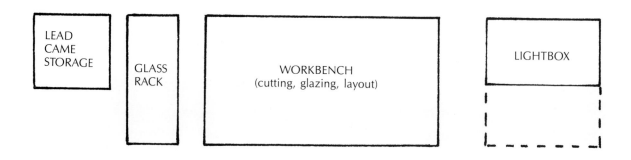

Figure 1 *Basic studio/workplace layout*

technically requires Council approval. It is recommended that this and all subsequent expansion schemes first be addressed to your local Council for official approval. Generally, the pursuit of craft type home activities is looked upon favourably by Councils, but it is always advisable to check before going ahead with any plans.

If you are working from home you will need to consider the following factors:
- Ease of customer parking.
- Clear access to your studio for members of the public.
- A professional visual presentation of your home studio when would-be customers call.
- A separate entrance for your studio so that potential customers don't have to skirt around the kids or the kitchen table to get into your workplace.

Generally speaking members of the public are not that keen on calling at private homes to see someone offering professional services such as leadlighting, although the more separate and self-contained your home workplace is, the greater chance you'll have of overcoming this problem.

Remember to make your home workplace *look* like a leadlight studio! Don't have lawnmowers and household junk cluttering up your space. Try and imagine that your work area is a commercial outlet and design and decorate it accordingly. First customer impressions are telling and many a potential client has been lost because the leadlighter's home workplace looked more like a den than a professional studio. See Figure 1.

Ideally your home workspace should be at the front of your house, or close to the main road access. This way the potential customer doesn't have to spend time wandering around your house or garden trying to guess where your studio is! Put studio signs in a prominent place to help callers find you quickly.

A business sign (needing Council approval) should be placed at the front of your house and should incorporate your business logo, name and contact telephone number.

While we're on the subject of telephones, remember that *all* business enquiries are potential customers. This is particularly true for home-based businesses where the telephone is the only initial point of customer contact, unlike a shop or commercial premises where clients often come in off the street to discuss their leadlight requirements.

It would be in your best interests, if you are conducting your business from home, to avail yourself of an answering machine so that *all* customer calls can be recorded and immediately followed up.

Unless they plan to move on to a purpose-built professional studio in the garden, most home-based leadlighters eventually expand into the commercial marketplace by taking a shop or commercial premises nearby.

The studio/shop

The public tends to equate success with exposure, such as working from a shop. However, you would be wise not to switch to a shop situation until you have regular customers and have built up some sort of continuity in your work load and banking habits. Shops cost money and you need to do your sums to ensure that you can survive the first twelve months, now that you are paying rent.

Moving into a shop/studio means that you will have to radically alter your work habits. Instead of being able to fit in your leadlighting at hours that suit you, you now have to set regular opening hours and be there!

Depending on your domestic situation it is still possible to operate a shop/studio but to restrict its opening hours to fit in with your personal life. You could, for example, initially open the shop only on weekends, thereby giving you most of the week at home.

The studio/shop should feature an interesting walk-in front area where your wares can be displayed for sale to the public. The photo shows a wide selection of leadlight shades

A workroom in your studio/shop (preferably at the rear) can be fitted out with tables and equipment for use by students at your private leadlight classes

A leadlight sculpture constructed from old found objects and entitled 'Guardians'

Assorted pieces of old iron and wood went into making this leadlight sculpture entitled 'Aefrika'

This leadlight sculpture makes use of an old cast iron frame to display the piece. The work is entitled 'White Owl' and is seen here in Togs Gallery, Castlemaine, Victoria

18

The leadlighter's workbench (right, foreground) is so positioned that customers coming in the shop door can immediately be served. Working in full view of the public also gives you a high profile

Perhaps you might consider getting a leadlight partner, or partners, to join you in the shop, each taking it in turns to staff it say two or three days a week, thereby sharing the time and the rent. Although the disadvantage in this would be that you would have to share the incoming leadlight work with the one or two others also working there, your savings in time and rent would balance this out.

Remember to advertise the fact that your services are now available through your new shop/studio; this is likely to bring in those potential customers who have been aware of your services previously, but were hesitant about calling at your home to find out more about getting leadlight work done.

If you do branch out into a shop/studio, try and find one that isn't too far from where you live. Time is valuable in any business and hours spent travelling to and from your place of work are wasted time.

When selecting premises try and keep in mind the following:

• Close proximity to a main road or public shopping/access area.
• Good front window space so that your wares/services are readily seen from the street.
• Rear lane access and readily available public parking space.
• Somewhere that has plenty of light and looks interesting and inviting.
• Premises that are slightly run down so that a favourable rental can be negotiated.
• Securing a long lease.

A shop/studio should be looked upon as a business investment in so far as, after a number of years of successful trading, the business can be sold as a going concern.

Your newly acquired shop/studio should be repainted in colours sympathetic to the sort of business you are conducting there, thereby adding to the venue's visual attractiveness to passersby.

4 WHICH DIRECTION – COMMERCIAL OR ART?

At some stage of their working lives most leadlighters will come face to face with the dilemma of creative intent, having to choose between leadlights as a commercial marketplace commodity and leadlights as art. Making the career decision about which road to pursue in the end comes down to personal choice and the individual's own attitude.

Generally speaking there is plenty of commercial work about in the marketplace and usually it is only the leadlighter's own ability to carry out the constant work which has to be considered.

Commercial leadlighting means literally that—being ready and able to do leadlights for a wide cross-section of the community with a heavy emphasis on the domestic side of the business, i.e. householders.

If you are quite happy to follow other's specific design and colour requirements (most householders approach leadlighters with definite designs and colours in mind, usually to suit their house decor) then this is the road for you.

Usually, unless you have developed a strong personal artistic approach to your work, you will not have a great deal of say when members of the public come to you to make them leadlights. Sometimes you can strike a domestic client who will let you have your artistic head in design and colour details but this is the exception rather than the rule.

To enter into commercial leadlighting is to face the same rules that apply to all other commercial household items—the product must be what the customer wants, it must be keenly priced, and it has to be made and installed as soon as possible!

Often the customer will want you to copy a leadlight design seen in a home decorating journal. At other times you might be expected to incorporate some personal feature into a panel, e.g. someone's initials worked into the overall design.

Commercial work will also have you making a lot of plain, diamond pane panels for kitchen or bureau use, as well as for bay windows and laundry areas.

In the end it takes a particular type of person to keep up with the never-ending stream of commercial jobs that

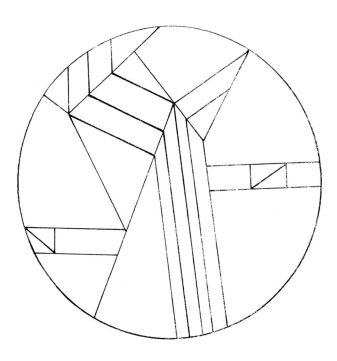

will walk into your studio. Such a person needs to be a very hard worker with an eye to making money from the profession. Also, such a person cannot afford to be anything less than enthusiastic about taking on anything and everything that turns up to be made.

As speed counts in commercial leadlighting the practitioner needs to develop considerable expertise in the cutting and construction side of the work as it is these areas that take the longest to do. The faster (and more efficient) one becomes at glass cutting and panel construction the sooner the job is completed and the next one can be started. Standards must, however, always remain high and thoroughly professional.

Turnover is the key to success in leadlighting on a commercial basis, as it is with almost everything manufactured and sold today.

As you become more skilled it is probably a good idea to employ a junior on a part-time basis, to help out with simple cutting jobs (such as clear glass diamond-panes) and puttying. The time you save by being able to hand these tasks over to someone else will enable you to devote your energies to more important work.

If this type of leadlighting operation sounds a little too narrow, artistically speaking, then chances are your creative spirit is making itself heard! And you might do well to consider a less commercial career in leadlighting.

Leadlights as an art medium ideally suits the person who has plenty of original design ideas and concepts and who finds it more important to express those ideas than to follow other's designs (which may be more conventional).

But be warned! Leadlighting as art will not bring you in as much money as a career in commercial work. And the road in art, as with all artistic fields, is long and hard. But take heart! At least you can be master of your own creative ideas and, with a little luck, score the odd artistic commission which satisfies both your creativity and the bank manager!

Often it is wise, at least in the initial stages of your career, to combine the two forms of the craft. Commercial leadlighting will help pay the bills and also enable you to produce those individual artistic leadlights which can be exhibited or displayed at galleries or exhibitions. The trick is, when combining both types of leadlighting, to allow yourself one or two days a week free of commercial work to devote entirely to your own creative leadlighting.

The temptation will be, because of the funds provided by the commercial side of your business, to let this side of things overflow into your own artistic time. This requires firm discipline and a conviction on your part that the one or two days a week spent working on your own

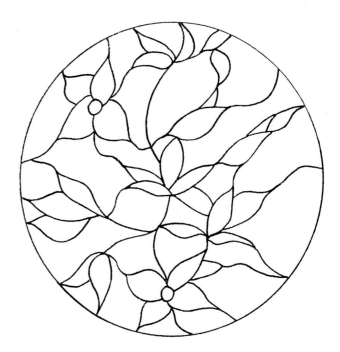

designs and ideas are sacrosanct and cannot be intruded upon. Once you have established a working pattern it will not present such a problem.

It is best if you think of the one or two days of private leadlight work as an investment for the future—something which may not return much in the way of funds yet, but which one day will.

If you are keen to pursue this art area you must stick to your weekly routine, and keep at it. Rome was not built in a day and this equally applies to gaining a reputation as an art leadlighter.

As your commercial business grows you will find that you will look forward greatly to that one or two days each week when you can retreat from the commercial pressures and enjoy yourself to pursue your own unique creative ideas in glass.

In time, as your name becomes known for your artistic work you will gradually start getting commissions in this area, where your individual artistic style is sought after and you have a completely free rein in all aspects of the work.

Long term, with any luck, the artistic side of your business will grow to the point where you can concentrate on it full-time, perhaps being able to hand over virtually all of your commercial leadlight work to your apprentice or part-time assistant who by this time should be experienced enough to eagerly take it on.

5 THE COMMERCIAL MARKETPLACE

Being willing and able to take on any and all commercial leadlight work will guarantee that you are going to be busy!

As mentioned in Chapter 4, if you are going to work commercially you would do well to find yourself an assistant who can do puttying and some of the more basic tasks to help you out. This way your design and client-contact time is freed up to enable you to secure more business.

You will be cutting the more complicated designs; as these will be your mainstay, financially speaking, with an assistant you will be able to get on with them uninterrupted.

Commercial leadlight work includes virtually any application for the use of leadlights that you can think of.

Domestic/household

This is a large and constant market which will probably always form the backbone of your business. If you are operating from a shop/studio you can expect domestic clients to come in off the street, either as curious passersby or as a result of seeing your leadlight advertisement in the local paper.

If you enjoy doing leadlights for houses make a feature of this sort of service in your advertising. Perhaps you could produce a flyer or small facts sheet or leaflet and have copies distributed to all householders in your immediate area.

Although there is a growing intolerance of junk mail you could overcome this by offering a 10–15% discount on their first window to all new customers brought in by the leaflet.

Most householders who have a leadlight made and installed will have a second or third panel made later on so your offer of a discount on the first panel will easily be repaid further down the track.

Remember also to take a stand in any (and all) local Home Shows or exhibitions/markets that might be held.

Personal representation at such functions is important in getting to meet prospective clients. And as previously mentioned, teaching leadlights, either privately from your studio or via the local Learning or Education Centre is another good way of getting your name known and meeting new customers.

It is important that you have some sort of photographic record of past domestic and/or commercial commissions to show clients when they come into your studio. One or two good quality photo albums displaying large colour photographs of your work is an ideal method of presentation. Remember to caption each job photo with location and panel size details and the date of installation. This way you gain workplace credibility and are perceived as having a good work record.

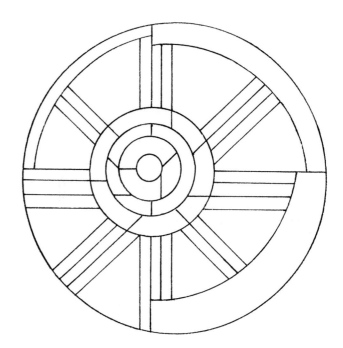

Kitchen manufacturers

As part of your business expansion visit the various kitchen manufacturers in your area, offering your leadlight services. Many manufacturers of commercial kitchens incorporate plain glass diamond-pane leadlights in their cupboards; this is the area you should target. The work is repetitious but securing a work contract with such a manufacturer assures you of another regular source of income. And diamond-pane work is something you can confidently pass over to your assistant to handle, from start to finish.

Kit homes/builders

Another market you should try and penetrate commercially lies with kit home suppliers and/or local builders. These days builders strive to make their homes or kits different from those of their competitors; what better way than by incorporating original leadlight work.

Perhaps you could offer an exclusive leadlight window in their particular house or kit model; by securing such an agreement more regular income is guaranteed. With such work it is important that the window you are offering is not too elaborate otherwise your price (to the builder) will be too high.

Remember you are entering the commercial marketplace where price and delivery time remain the two most important factors.

Commercial businesses

Restaurants, beauty salons, motels, guest houses, hotels—just some of the potential customers waiting for your leadlights to brighten up their places a little!

Make it a point to pay a personal visit to each and every such establishment in your immediate area. Take your photo books with you; pay particular attention to each business you visit so that you can point out any windows in the premises that are particularly suitable for leadlighting.

Sell yourself and your work and, if need be, offer special 'first panel' discounts to clinch the deal. Restaurants and upmarket hotels are particularly suitable for leadlight work and chances are that once you have one of your panels installed the owners will want you to make another one or two, or maybe even three!

Lighting shops

Target lighting shops to see if they would be interested in stocking a range of leadlight lampshades. These need not be too complicated but must be attractive and in fashionable colours.

Offer the shop an 'exclusive' on your leadlight light shades, perhaps stocking six different designs to start with to gauge public reaction.

After you have made a few shade sales you will soon be able to see which of your designs are popular and can then concentrate on making these.

Craft shops/tourist outlets

If your assistant has any spare time (in between puttying and cutting out diamond-panes) you could get him/her to cut a range of simple (but original) leadlight mobiles and suncatchers. These can be made from scrap glass and copperfoil and placed in (or sold direct to) craft shops in your area.

If your region is a tourist spot you could make the glass mobiles with a local theme, thereby aiding their ready sale as souvenirs. Leadlight mirrors are another good retail item for such shops; these also could feature local tourist themes.

Repairs

Repairing broken leadlights forms another income-producing branch of your business. Repairs are covered fully in Chapter 7.

6 LEADLIGHTS AS ART

Leadlighting is a medium that lends itself well to the area of art work.

The key factors in presenting your work as art lie in your own creativity and imagination. Both these areas have to be highly developed in a leadlight artist; someone working in this field needs also to be both original and skilled in the mechanics of panel presentation and display.

It goes without saying that experience, both in designing and making leadlights, is vital before entering the area of art pieces.

Getting started

One good way of starting out is to visit your local art gallery and let the director know about you and your work. It would help if you also took along a rough outline of what your proposed exhibition leadlight art piece/s will look like. You may perhaps have in mind a series of panels that are part of an overall concept, e.g. summer, autumn, winter, spring.

Take rough colour drawings to your meeting with the gallery director. This will show that you have already put work into your project; from your roughs the director will readily be able to gauge the suitability of your work for exhibition.

Leadlighting has still not really cracked the art circuit and you may have to convince the gallery director that the medium deserves 'art' exposure.

In any gallery situation your leadlights (if they are

hanging panels) should ideally be hung over windows directly facing the outside light. This provides the most dramatic lighting for your work which is immediately visible to everyone visiting the gallery.

Sometimes display type windows are not available; in such cases you will have to provide some sort of artificial illumination for your work. This can be in the form of elevated lightboxes where your panel is displayed in front of the box which is lighted from behind by fluorescent tubes.

Another, slightly less successful, way of featuring leadlights in a gallery situation is to floodlight them from

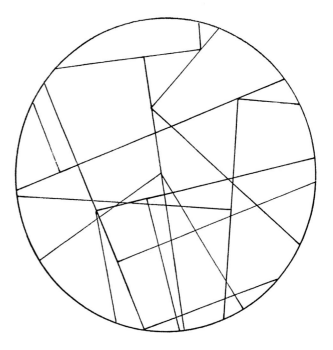

behind. If this method is to be used you will need to find a relatively dark corner of the gallery floor space in which to site your leadlight so that when floodlit the panel is illuminated amid the gloom.

Under no circumstances should you allow a gallery to display your leadlight work flat against a wall or display stand so that no light is permitted through the piece.

It is important that galleries understand the difference between exhibiting leadlights and, say, conventional paintings. With a leadlight the work *becomes the light* itself and therefore must be in front of some form of strong light.

Most commercial galleries charge artistis at least 30% commission for selling their work—something to ponder when you come to price your art piece!

The art circuit is all about exhibition credibility, so it is important that you make a photographic and documented record of any and all exhibitions you have of your work.

After several successful local gallery exhibitions it would be a good idea to progress to a larger venue. Perhaps your area has a regional art gallery? If so you should visit it and talk to its director, showing your previous exhibition documentation, and then try and arrange for an exhibition of your work there. New exhibitions call for new ideas and new works so you should have an outline already drawn up for your regional gallery show.

Exhibition in a regional art gallery has more clout than smaller local exhibitions; you should actively engage in generating maximum publicity for your work when this exhibition is on. This should include contacting all local and regional newspapers, television and radio stations to cover your exhibition. Always make sure you have an artist's profile available at any exhibition; this is a printed sheet listing your art background with full details of all previous exhibitions, and is made available to all visitors to the gallery showing your work.

Getting your name and work *known* is vitally important to success in any area of art, and leadlighting is no exception.

Presentation

Novel approaches to art capture the public's attention and it would be well to think of new ways of displaying art leadlights for this very reason.

Apart from standard lightbox type display panels leadlights lend themselves extremely well to sculpture. Sculpture is growing in popularity with the public; by combining leadlights with this medium you project your pieces into a three-dimensional realm.

Any sculpture you do should be designed to form an interesting display vehicle for your leadlight work, e.g. a large, free-standing pyramid made either of angle iron or wood, its sides in-filled with creative leadlights and the whole lit from inside by masked fluorescent lights. Old iron makes interesting sculpture and can be combined with leadlight panels to form a striking art object. Keep an eye out for interesting old items (ideally with holes or openings already in them) that could be reconstucted into unique display frames for your leadlight work.

Think also of ways that your leadlight sculpture might be used. Perhaps a leadlighted pyramid could form an interesting courtyard art piece? Or maybe an old iron and leadlight sculpture would make a dynamic interior light?

Consider the use of art leadlight screens as another avenue for your work. Such pieces could be used as room dividers or features; they could be made from wood or some other lightweight material such as brass or copper. Their designs should be daring and original with no two being the same. Remember you are now in the area of art where originality and individuality count.

Leadlighted screens make ideal gallery exhibition pieces and give the artist great scope for creating new themes.

The business connection

At the end of an exhibition you will usually find yourself left with unsold works. What to do with them? Some can be re-exhibited in the future, but others should be sold off.

If you also run your own shop/studio you can place your unsold pieces there for sale. However, it is probably a better idea to have a working arrangement with a high quality gift shop or interior decorator to sell those exhibition pieces you no longer want to hang on to. This way your art work reaches the general public while also bringing in valuable sales which can help finance your next gallery exhibition.

Another art business connection you should endeavour to make is with architects. Make yourself and your work known to the architects in your region and always remember to invite them to your gallery exhibitions. Making solid connections with architects who appreciate and use art in their buildings is a big bonus for any creative leadlighter.

Advertising in suitable art and architectural journals is another way of keeping your name and work in a high profile mode in this area. Art commissions for private residences, exhibition halls, upmarket restaurants and public buildings should come your way in time as you and your work become better known.

This leadlight hanging light was commissioned by a Bathurst NSW customer for his home

Left: This leadlight sculpture was exhibited in the Regional Art Gallery in Orange NSW before it was donated to the Blue Mountains Tourist Authority for permanent display at its Echo Point Tourist Information Centre

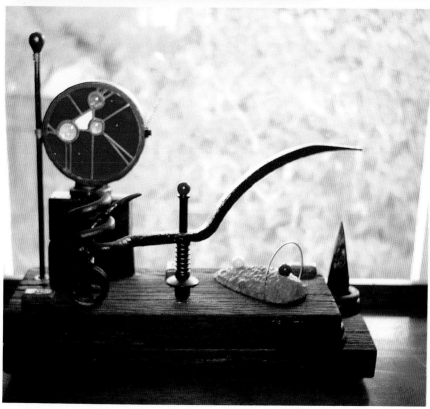

A leadlight sculpture entitled 'Signals', made from found wooden and iron objects. Now in a private collection in the Victorian town of Castlemaine

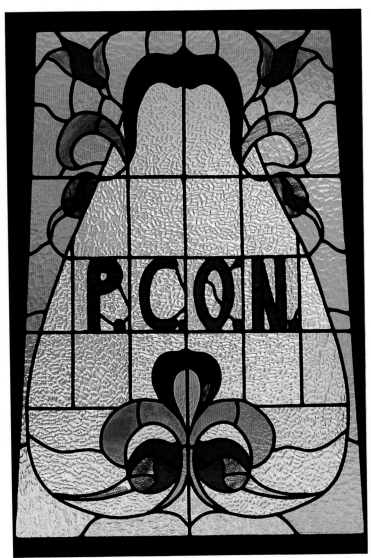

This door panel was commissioned for a solicitor in Katoomba NSW. The client's initials are incorporated in the design

This small panel was made for sale to the public in a shop situation

Another 'one-off' small leadlight panel made for general sale to the public

This octagonal panel was commissioned for a client's house in Medlow Bath NSW. The leadlight was installed in a wall at the front of the weatherboard house, adding more light to the entry area

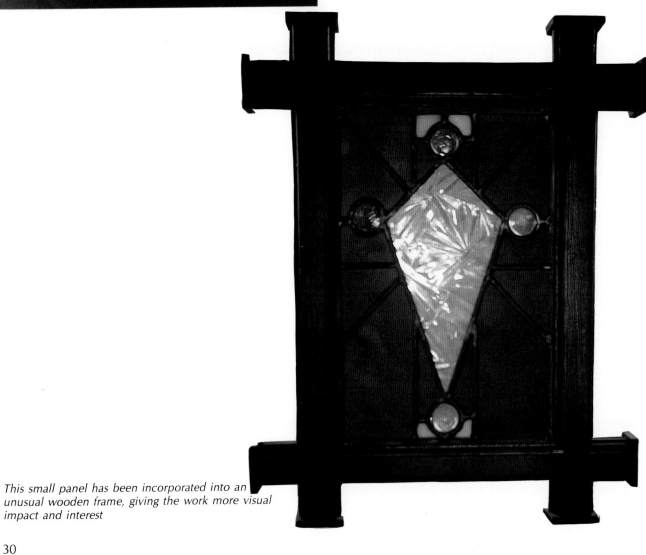

This small panel has been incorporated into an unusual wooden frame, giving the work more visual impact and interest

7 REPAIRING LEADLIGHTS

A very useful avenue of extra income for your leadlight business is doing repairs. This means new leadlights as well as old ones, as the technique for repairs is the same.

If your shop/studio sign clearly states that you also do leadlight repairs you will find no shortage of people bringing in old or damaged windows for you to fix. These 'mobile' repairs should always be carried out with the panel lying flat on the workbench.

If the window you are fixing has several cracks and requires extensive restoration always remember to first clean the glass and lead thoroughly (before you quote!) so you can see *exactly* what has to be done.

Often the tiny fractures which occur at lead joints in old panels can go undetected under layers of dust and grime.

Panels have a habit of 'spreading' when you are repairing them, sometimes resulting in the restored leadlight ending up a centimetre or two larger than it was made and making refitting into its original opening difficult. Spreading can be prevented while repairs are being made by putting horseshoe nails hard up against all the border edges before you start, to lock the panel together, thereby keeping its size constant.

Mobile leadlight repairs include virtually anything that can be easily handled—such as small windows, cabinets, front and back doors, kitchen cupboards.

Repairing leadlights is a very time-consuming task and serious consideration should always be given to the extent of the restoration work required *before* quoting customers.

Straightforward repairs

Sometimes you will be asked to repair a window which has half-a-dozen or so clean cracks in the panes.

This type of repair is quite straightforward and simply requires that the restorer disguise the cracks (on both sides) by covering them with a length of normal lead came from which the heart and one side have been removed, leaving a rounded flat strip. This single strip of

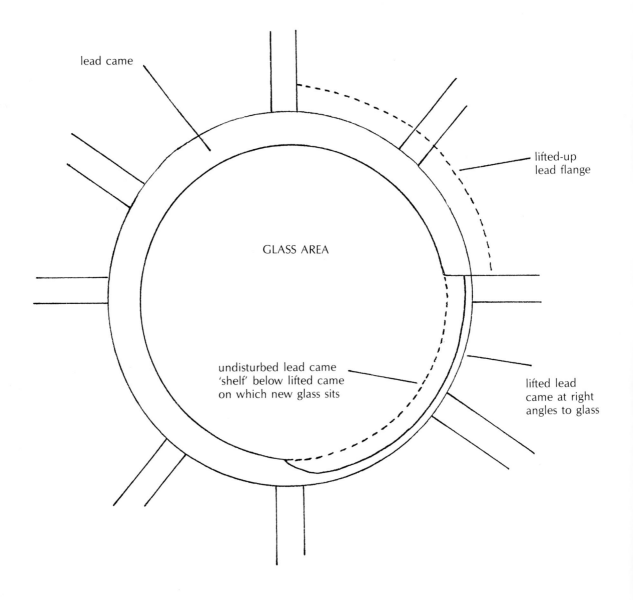

lead came

lifted-up
lead flange

GLASS AREA

undisturbed lead came
'shelf' below lifted came
on which new glass sits

lifted lead
came at right
angles to glass

Figure 1

lead is then cut to length to cover the crack and soldered onto the nearest lead came.

Make sure if the glass crack curves that you follow it by slightly curving the strip of covering lead.

When all the cracks in the panel have been successfully covered on both sides, putty underneath each of the lead cover strips as this helps to both secure and weatherproof the repair.

Another form of simple leadlight repair is when the panel to be fixed has cracks or breaks located near the outside border area. With the panel on a flat bench use your lead knife and carefully cut through the border edges closest to the break. Turn the panel over and repeat the process on the other side. Remove the border lead strip and secure the panel firmly to the workbench with horseshoe nails hard against the leaded edges.

It is essential to be gentle when removing broken glass from panels as old putty becomes very hard and sometimes tends to pull away and disturb the adjoining leaded glass sections as a pane is being removed.

If you also have to remove any good pieces of glass to get to your repair, always remember to thoroughly clean them of old putty so that when they are returned to the came they will sit properly in the channels.

After the broken glass has been removed clear out the channels in the lead came with your lead knife, removing any old putty or glass fragments. Place the new piece of glass directly over the opening to be filled and trace over the lead, onto the glass, the came-edged shape below.

If the replacement glass is very dark you will need to put the whole panel on top of a lightbox to clearly see the lead came shape below. Sometimes the piece of removed border lead has to be put back so that an accurate picture can be made of the shape to be cut.

Remember to cut the new glass to *slightly less* than the centre of the came below so that it will fit properly.

It is not uncommon to have to groze the new piece of glass slightly to fit the old opening.

After all the broken glass has been replaced simply rejoin and solder the border lead, re-putty all disturbed areas of the panel (on both sides) and the job is done.

More complicated repairs

If you get a repair where most of the broken pieces are located in the central area of the panel you will have to take the panel apart—literally.

Before you do this you must make a copy of the original panel. Place a piece of white paper on top of the panel and, using a black crayon, rub all over the leadlines, borders included.

You end up with a crayon impression clearly showing the window leadlines beneath—somewhat like a church brass rubbing.

Number each piece of glass on the original panel and on the rubbed impression.

Doing this gives you a visual record of where each piece of glass belongs—important for reconstructing the panel *exactly* after repairs have been made.

Always remember to carefully measure the exact dimensions of the panel before you start dismantling it so that this size is maintained following repairs.

Using your lead knife sever the panel leads horizontally (on both sides) so that the panel is literally cut in half.

Once you have separated the top half of the panel from the bottom half you are free to take out and replace the central broken glass and any damaged lead needing attention.

Once all the breaks have been fixed, rejoin the panel, firmly securing it on the workbench with horseshoe nails against all outside edges. Check the repairs and leading with the rubbed impression to make sure that the new work is faithful to the original. Also, ensure you measure (and adjust if necessary) the reassembled panel so that its dimensions exactly match its original size.

The panel can now be soldered and puttied up in the normal way.

On-site repairs

When you are called upon to repair leadlights on site, where the broken panel cannot be taken away to be fixed, another repair technique is used.

Basically, this method involves lifting up the top flanges of the lead came (on one side only) so that they stick up at right angles to the glass around each break needing repair.

Every lead joint around each piece of broken glass is first severed with the lead knife (on one side only) and then the lead came gently lifted up, leaving a neat lead shelf below for the new glass to sit on.

A pair of square, smooth-jawed pliers is best for this method of repair. *Never* use grozing pliers to lift the lead came as they tend to score and crush the lead, making it lumpy and disfigured.

Once the broken glass pieces have been removed run your lead knife along the bottom ledges of the lifted came to completely remove all traces of old putty and glass.

Each empty hole must now be refilled with new glass cut to size. With an ink pen trace the size of each piece of new glass over the specific hole it has to fit, remembering to cut almost up to the heart line of the lead below. New pieces may have to be wiggled or grozed slightly to fit.

Once all the new glass has been fitted, carefully bend down the lifted lead came, using the edge of your lead knife, so that it covers the outer edges of the glass beneath. The butting leads should now all be soldered in the normal way.

If any sections of the previously lifted came still look a little uneven after they have been pushed back down, you can remedy this by going over the rough sections several times with your lead knife.

The panel can now be puttied up on both sides.

When doing on-site leadlight repairs it is usual to lift up the lead came on the *inside* of the installation. This is especially important for any windows facing the weather as it leaves the exterior leading undisturbed, thereby maintaining its weather seal.

Sagging panels

On occasions you will be asked to fix a panel that has sagged (either outward or inwards), resulting in it becoming rattly and floppy.

If the sag isn't too bad you can sometimes ease the panel back into the vertical position by placing two exact-size pieces of chipboard front and back against the panel, and gently pressing against them, sandwiching the sagging panel between.

Any fractured panel joints (or broken/cracked glass) can then be made good and the window reputtied.

If the straightened panel is a large one (more than 1.2 m or 4' high) or is part of a door or other installation subject to constant movement, it should be further strengthened by adding steel bars to it.

These are attached to the panel by copper loops which tie the window to the bar whose ends are securely slotted into the surrounding wooden frame.

If you are presented with a window which has sagged badly and has no strength left in it, the only course of action is to completely dismantle it and re-lead the entire panel as new.

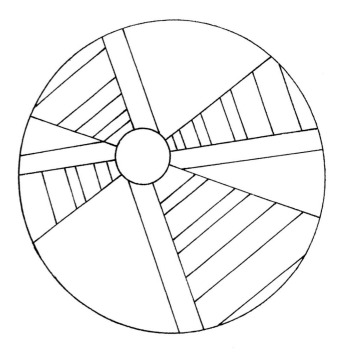

8 INSTALLING LEADLIGHTS

When you design and make leadlights for a living you will also have to become adept at installing your work. Some professionals employ glaziers to do this work on their behalf but for someone running a small business it pays to handle all new work installations personally.

Set aside one day a week as your installation day so that your studio work time is not interrupted daily.

Leadlights can be installed directly into existing window frames or doors, old or new, or can be mounted in a separate frame fastened in front of an existing clear glass window.

Tools

A wooden mallet, a sharp chisel, a small old plane, some spare border lead came, some masking tape, a flat scraper, a pair of pliers and work gloves are the basic items required to remove old glass from an existing window frame, and to fit new leadlights.

Installation in existing frames

First make sure that the window rebate is deep enough to take the new leadlight. If it isn't deep enough, you will have to carefully chisel out the rebate to increase its depth.

Next, carefully remove the old glass from the frame.

This operation is begun with a chisel and wooden mallet, chipping away all existing glazing putty (or removing wooden beading if the frame has been finished this way) until you reach the glass.

If the glass has been puttied you will usually find some glazing brads (small flat nails) along each edge of the pane. Remove these with pliers and carefully lift the old glass out of the frame.

If the sheet of glass to be removed is quite large it will pay you to attach masking tape to one side in a large X, thus ensuring that the glass will not shatter over you should you accidentally crack it.

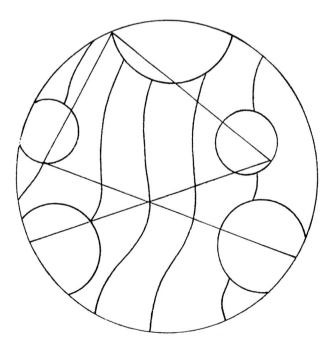

It should be noted that the putty in old windows can be extremely hard and care and patience is required to remove it.

If you are removing glass from a modern installation, chances are it will have been siliconed in, which greatly increases the risk of the glass breaking. Take the precaution of taping the panel before attempting its removal.

When doing this kind of work wear a pair of work gloves to protect your fingers and hands from possible cuts.

If the old glass has stuck around the edges of the frame you will have to gently insert a putty knife or flat scraper between the wooden frame and the glass to help prise it free.

Once the old glass has been successfully removed from the frame take a broad chisel and carefully scrape around the rebate to remove all traces of old putty or silicone.

If the new panel is a fraction too short for the frame its height can be raised a few millimetres by placing some flattened border lead came at either end and in the middle for correct support. If your leadlight panel is a fraction too large for the frame it can be adjusted by trimming off some of the outside border lead with an old plane or shears. Ideally, of course, the new leadlight panel should sit inside the framed rebate without any adjustments being necessary.

Once you have sized the leadlight for the frame remove it and apply clear silicone (or putty if you prefer) all around the window rebate where the panel is going to sit.

Be careful with silicone—if you use too much it will ooze all over the edges of the panel when you install it.

Carefully place the leadlight into the prepared frame rebate, easing it firmly in so that its edges make a firm seal with the silicone or putty you have applied.

When the panel is sitting squarely in the frame secure

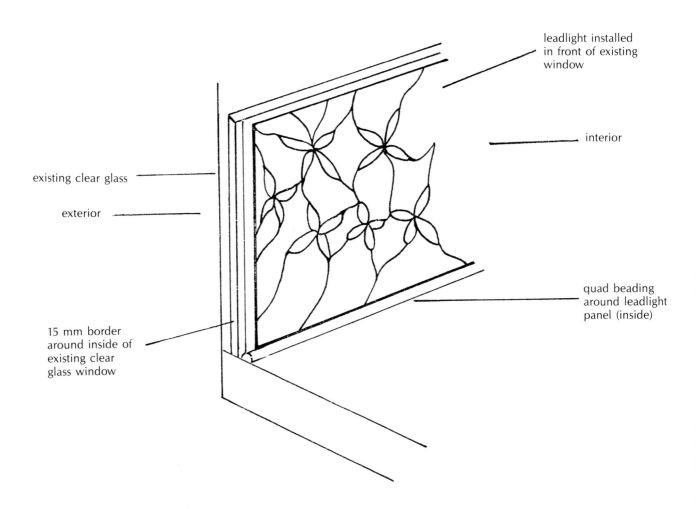

existing clear glass

exterior

15 mm border around inside of existing clear glass window

leadlight installed in front of existing window

interior

quad beading around leadlight panel (inside)

Figure 1

36

it at top, bottom and sides, using long blue cut tacks. Gently hammer the tacks through the very outside edges of the border lead, making sure you don't strike the inside flange or surrounding glass. A broad-ended nail punch is best used for this delicate operation.

When securing the panel's edges with tacks always make sure that you choose a point on the border leads where an inside lead joins, for additional support. If you attempt to tack on the border next to a long run of unsupported glass you will almost certainly crack it.

When you have finished securing the panel in the frame go around with the silicone gun again and seal the outside frame edges of the leadlight.

If you are glazing a panel into an old style frame that was previously puttied you will have to finish off by puttying in the panel. This is done by pushing in putty over the silicone and finishing off smoothly using a putty knife or a broad chisel.

With a modern window frame you probably won't have to putty it at all, just re-fit the four pieces of wooden border quad directly against and over the edges of the siliconed-in panel.

Installation in front of existing windows

In those cases where it is inconvenient or impractical to install a leadlight panel directly into an existing frame (e.g. where a window is several stories from the ground and is glazed from the outside), the panel can be mounted either *in front* of the clear glass window pane or *over* the opening itself.

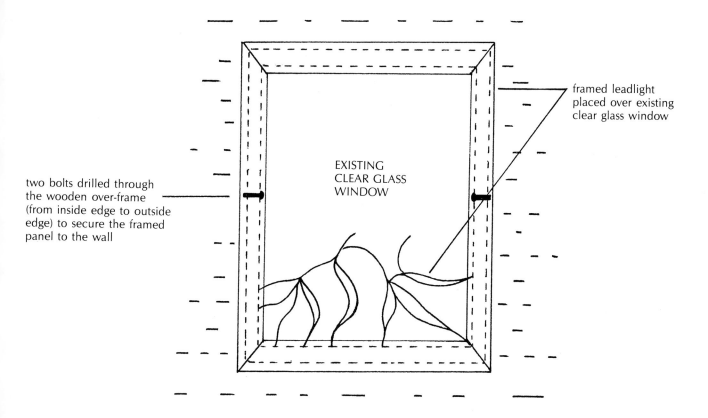

framed leadlight placed over existing clear glass window

EXISTING CLEAR GLASS WINDOW

two bolts drilled through the wooden over-frame (from inside edge to outside edge) to secure the framed panel to the wall

Figure 2

To install a leadlight in front of an existing sheet of glass simply nail and butt end four pieces of wood 15 mm × 15 mm to the *insides* of the existing window frame, leaving a 15 mm air space between the original sheet of clear glass and the leadlight being installed. See Figure 1.

Remember to thoroughly clean the existing window pane first!

When you have done this install the leadlight panel inside the frame against the four lengths of wood, and finish off by fixing a mitred wooden beading all around the panel on the viewing side, thus effectively double glazing the window.

Installation over existing windows

To install a leadlight over an existing clear glass window you will have to make a large wooden frame for the panel to sit in, similar to a picture frame. See Figure 2.

The wooden frame must be solid and strong enough to take the weight of the leadlight.

Glaze the panel into this frame in the normal way.

To install this over an existing window drill bolt holes in the centre of the sides of the frame (horizontally, from the inside edge of the frame through to the outside edge) and through into the wall. Anchor the panel to the surface using bolts.

This method allows the panel to be removed easily for cleaning or repair later on.

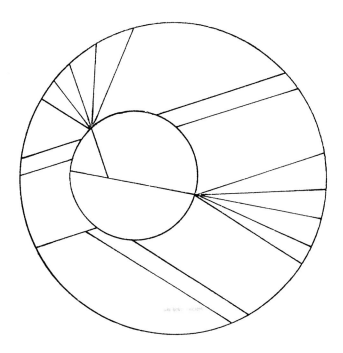

This front door panel was commissioned for installation in a renovated nineteenth century cottage in Daylesford, Victoria

A small panel commissioned for use in a renovated cottage in Chewton, Victoria, as a bedroom feature window

This three-piece work was commissioned for the Echo Point Tea Rooms tourist complex at Echo Point, Katoomba NSW

One of many leadlights commissioned by the Central Springs Inn, Daylesford, Victoria, for use throughout the tourist complex

9 BECOMING A STOCKIST

So, now you have your own shop/studio and are starting to make a steady return from designing and making leadlights, as well as teaching the craft in a back room of your premises.

You have probably worked out an arrangement with a local, larger leadlight studio (and stockist) whereby you can purchase glass and lead for yourself at special rates. But you're starting to find that students' demands for glass, lead and tools are eating into your own supplies. As well you are getting more and more people coming in off the street wanting to buy various leadlight materials and asking you for the latest design books...

And you can't say 'no' to these requests because you need the customer goodwill...

What to do? All this customer servicing is starting to erode your own work time, necessitating many trips to your local friendly leadlight supplier. Supplying your own leadlight students and drop-in hobbyists with glass, materials and books you've managed to obtain at special rates still shows you a profit—but only just.

Faced with this situation it is time to take the next step in becoming a professional leadlighter and become a stockist yourself. By doing this you can offer all your customers an extensive range of leadlight materials at a price that suits them, and you, from the comfort of your own shop.

As well, becoming a stockist means that you can more keenly price your own leadlight commissions as you are using glass and lead obtained at wholesale prices.

It is quite normal to increase your drop-in customers many times over once you become a stockist as your shop/studio soon becomes a focal point for a wide range of people in your area interested in the craft of leadlights.

Another of the advantages in becoming a stockist of leadlight materials is that you can use the stocked books, tools and accessories to dress up the front window space of your premises, thereby providing an eye-catching display for passersby.

Anyone with a registered leadlight business is eligible to become a stockist. Currently there is a minimum start-up order of $1000 from wholesalers.

Most metropolitan areas are serviced by leadlight wholesalers' own delivery vehicles and a courier service is available to country stockists.

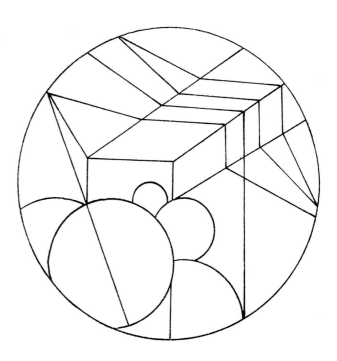

Located in a convenient corner of your shop/studio the glass rack carries an extensive range of leadlight glass in all colours and textures for sale to the public

When you become a leadlight stockist you can decorate the front area of your shop/studio with all the tools of the trade. Pictured here are leadlight books, tools, and a wide range of associated equipment

Suppliers

The following suppliers are involved in supplying stockists with leadlight products for resale:

Victoria
The Melbourne Glass Centre
12–14 Ceylon Street
Nunawading Vic. 3131
Phone: (03) 894-2083
Contact: David Edwards, Sean O'Leary

New South Wales
Glo-rite Glass
Unit 6/2 Burrows Road
St Peters NSW 2044
Phone: (02) 550-1688
Contact: Stuart Dunn

Queensland
The Leadlight Suppliers
PO Box 529
Redbank Plains Qld 4301
Phone: (07) 290-2824
Contact: Kathleen Henry

Townsville Stained Glass
PO Box 528
Townsville Qld 4810
Phone: (07) 771-3449
Contact: Bob Constantine

Western Australia
Colonial Stained Glass
608 Hay Street
Jolimont WA 6014
Phone: (09) 383-7944
Contact: Ian Dickson

South Australia
The Adelaide Glass Centre
20 College Road
Kent Town SA 5067
Phone: (08) 363-0766
Contact: Vince Rushby

Tasmania
Tasmania Stained Glass
'Blenheim', High Street
Evandale Tas 7212
Phone: (003) 91-8171
Contact: Robert Clarke

New Zealand
Leadlight & Lace
116 Vanguard Street
Nelson NZ
Phone: (0011) 64 3 548 0243
Contact: Malcolm McDonald

A Touch of Glass Ltd
670 Mt Albert Road
Three Kings, Auckland NZ
Phone: (0011) 64 9 625 9466
Contact: John Jones

10 SOME HINTS ON THE BUSINESS

After spending sixteen years as a designer and maker of original leadlight windows one learns some dos and don'ts of the trade. Having this information can make your life a great deal easier and also help to ensure that your leadlight business flourishes and continues to prosper. Much of your time as a leadlighter involves meeting (and motivating) people-customers, and a good manner is very important in this area.

Keep the following in mind in your day-to-day business operations:

Dos

1. Get it right *the first time!*
This applies to every aspect of leadlighting, from initial measurements, to design and assembly, right through to panel installation.

Care and attention to detail is vitally important in this profession and mistakes made early in the panel production process will come back to haunt you later!

Sloppy workmanship, poor design and bad colour choice are all hallmarks of the second-rate leadlighter, and will soon put you out of business.

2. Always present yourself and your work professionally
Make your studio/shop feel (and look) like a creative work place, somewhere where customers can get inspired along with you.

Make sure your presentation photo albums are always up to date, including your latest commissions to show potential customers.

3. Be positive at all times when dealing with customers
This personal attribute is a business asset and should be cultivated so that you are able to actively contribute creative ideas and options when talking with potential customers.

Be positive too about your prices.

Usually people don't mind paying for quality and originality and it's up to you to get this message across to customers *right from the start.*

4. Be efficient always
'Efficient' also means 'reliable'. If you take a leadlight

commission on and set a completion and installation date, *stick to it!*

There is nothing more irritating for customers than to be put off for another week or three because of personal inefficiency on the part of the leadlighter.

It is always a sound idea to add another week or so to your expected completion/installation time so that you have a few spare days up your sleeve should an unexpected emergency arise.

If you make a time to go and visit a potential customer for a business meeting make sure you are there when you said you would be. If you fail to turn up or are late for the scheduled home visit chances are you will lose a potential leadlight job *and* your name will immediately be put about as someone who is both unreliable and unprofessional.

5. Keep getting publicity for your work

It is important to keep your name and business in the public eye. As you complete interesting or special leadlight projects make sure you contact your local or regional newspaper so that they can run a small photo-story on the work.

You may have completed a large project for a domestic dwelling or perhaps a well-known restaurant. Take photographs of your work and send them (with captions or a small story) to suitable decor or trade publications. Most clients are happy to have their leadlights featured in this way but it is always a good idea to ask their permission first.

All this will add to your public exposure and help promote your business.

6. Secure a job deposit

It is always a good idea to secure a deposit from clients on each new leadlight job. This should be requested only after the design has been seen and approved by the customer. Usually an advance customer deposit totalling one-third of the final job price is sufficient.

Securing such a deposit means you are paid straight-away for your design work and the customer is financially committed to the job.

It has been known for difficult customers to suddenly change their minds about having a leadlight made—this when the hapless leadlighter has just spent two days making the panel! Obtaining your initial job deposit helps to cover you for such an occurrence and also gives you some working capital to proceed with the job.

Naturally enough a receipt must be issued for a deposit; this can be done immediately the design has been sighted and approved by the client.

7. Protect your original designs

It is important that you *never leave original designs with a customer or client* so that they can 'make up their minds' at leisure.

There really is no need to leave your designs with customers; it is up to you to negotiate a mutually suitable time when you can meet and discuss the designs.

A leadlighter should always be present when his/her designs are being considered because customers usually have certain questions (e.g. colour choice, design suitability, visual impact when installed) pertaining to the design which *only* a professional leadlighter can answer satisfactorily.

The danger you face by leaving 'undeposited' original designs with clients is that they may decide (in your absence) not to proceed with the job, perhaps after showing your design to another leadlighter (or amateur glass worker) who has offered to do the job more cheaply, copying your design!

Remember that your designs are original works; until they have been approved and paid for by the client they must be held by you at all times.

All your original designs should be inscribed with the copyright sign (C with a circle around it) and your name and the year clearly written inside.

The design remains yours under law even when you have completed and installed the leadlight. However, it is best not to make any more leadlights from it, thereby retaining one-off exclusivity for clients.

Don'ts

1. Don't ever take on a job you can't comfortably handle

If you are presented with a very large job, or one that requires expertise beyond your experience (e.g. the complete restoration of a nineteenth century stained glass church window), *never* take on the job. It is almost inevitable that you will become hopelessly bogged down in circumstances beyond your control, resulting in a business disaster and your immediate demise in the leadlight business.

In such circumstances it is better to act as a go-between and secure the services of others more experienced (or with a bigger studio team) and able to handle that type of work.

Chances are you will still be able to do some of the work, perhaps negotiating with whoever does the job some sort of sub-contracting deal whereby you get a certain amount of glass work to handle, leaving them to carry out the lion's share of the project.

It is always a good idea to have a working relationship with another leadlighter in your area so that if you do become snowed under with work you can delegate some of the load to them.

Such an arrangement gives you added flexibility in the workplace and also helps to build good business connections.

2. Don't undercharge for your work

Most leadlighters starting out work on a minimum charge, taking comfort in having actually made a leadlight for someone—even if it was for a relative. When you start making leadlights for a living this sort of attitude has to change, otherwise you will soon go broke!

Make enquiries around the other leadlighters in your region to find out what their minimum square metre charges are and use this average price as your charge guide.

If you are particularly gifted at design, and your work is highly original and dynamic, you can reasonably be expected to charge accordingly—but always bear in mind that your service has to operate in the marketplace where average prices usually prevail.

Work out your minimum charge (for straightforward jobs such as clear diamond-pane panels) and then vary it upwards according to the types of jobs you handle.

For example, a series of individually designed, original feature panels for, say, an upmarket restaurant or gallery would necessarily demand a higher fee.

Also, take note of the occasional price rises in the materials you use (lead, glass, etc.) as these have to be passed on to the client, as in any other type of business enterprise.

3. Don't sacrifice quality for quantity

Sometimes, when the pressure is on and you have a long list of leadlight jobs ahead of you, the temptation arises to rush work through in order to keep to deadlines.

Don't do it!

Far better, if you find yourself overloaded, to pass some of the work out to another leadlighter in your area. Leadlights should never be rushed, either in the glass cutting or in the construction process.

A consistent, high quality is important in all the work you do and your customers (and your own reputation) demand that this work ethic is firmly adhered to at all times.

4. Don't use second-rate glass

Using second-rate or cheap glass in your leadlights might save you money but it will also get you a reputation as being second-rate.

Good leadlights demand quality glass in their construction and using the best should become one of your business hallmarks.

5. Don't settle for bad designs

Sometimes a customer will want you to make a leadlight from a design they have already decided upon. If the required design is dull or plainly uninspiring, it is up to you, as a professional, to offer to make subtle changes to improve it.

Bear in mind that most clients are not experts in the field of design and usually will be only too happy to go along with your suggestions.

By modifying and improving such a design you are merely exercising your creative control over the job to everyone's benefit!

Bad design simply should never be duplicated or, better still, never done in the first place.

11 TWELVE NEW LEADLIGHT DESIGNS

turn page this way

50

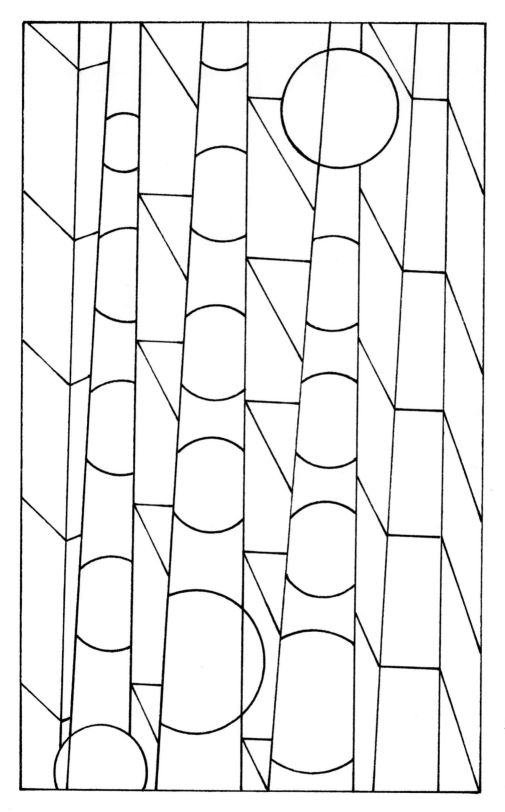

turn page this way

51

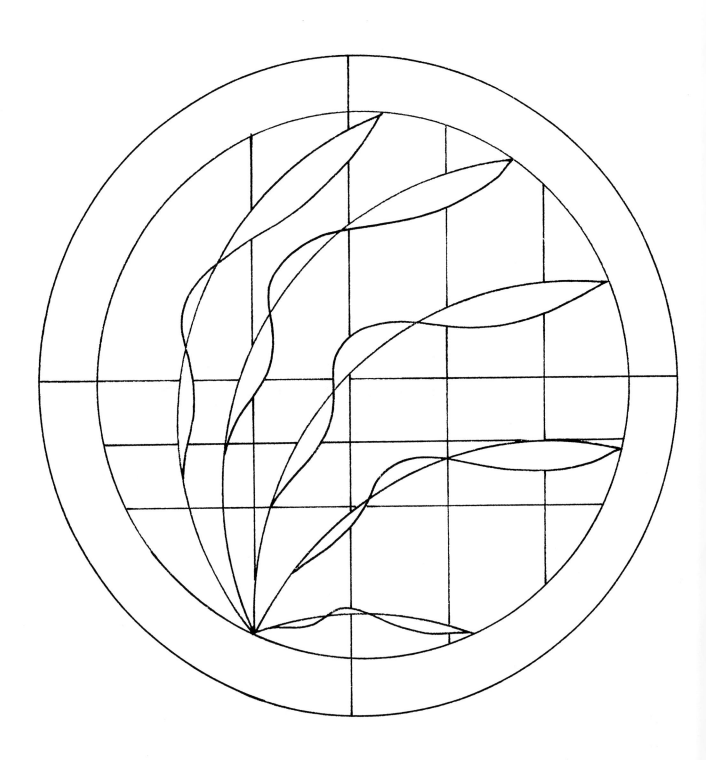

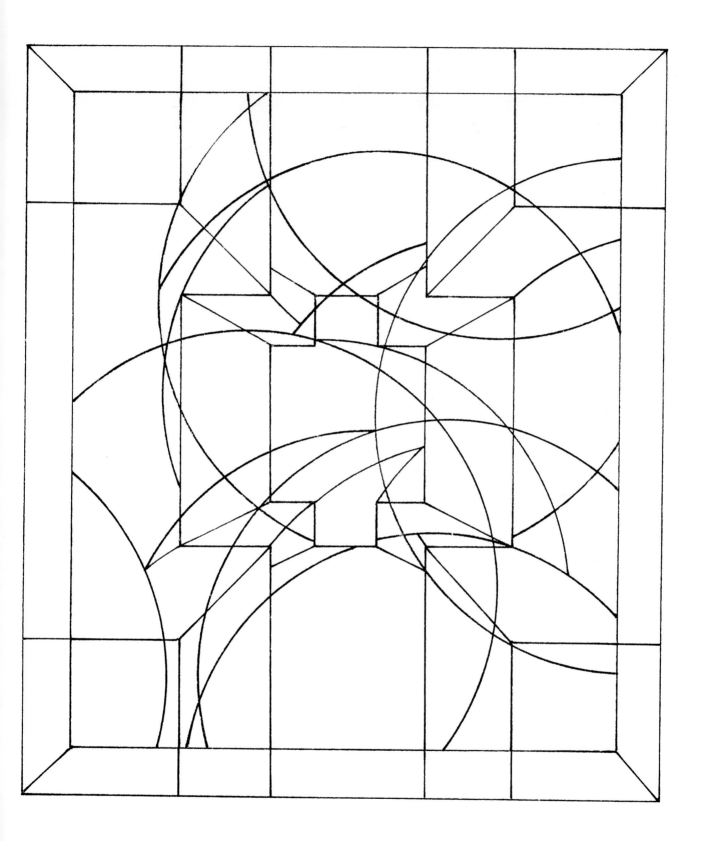

55

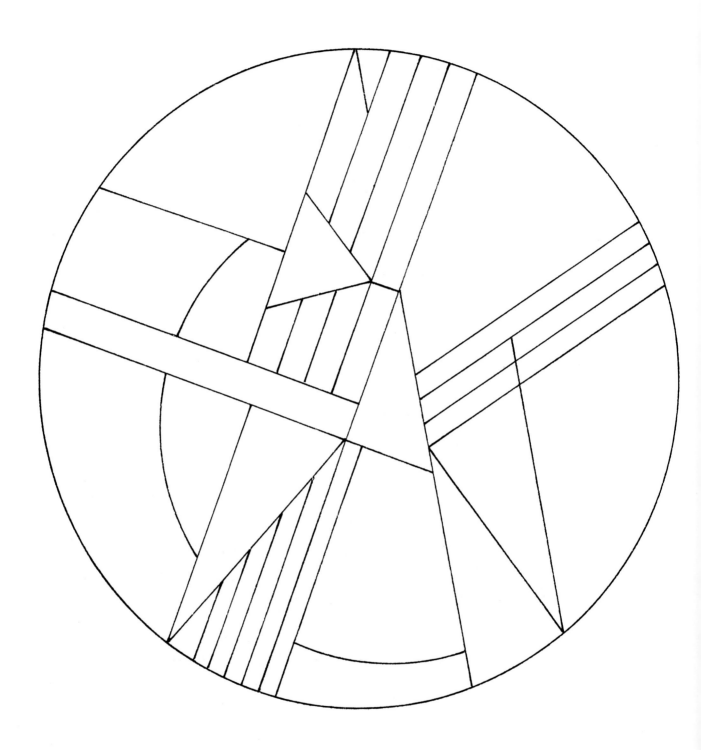

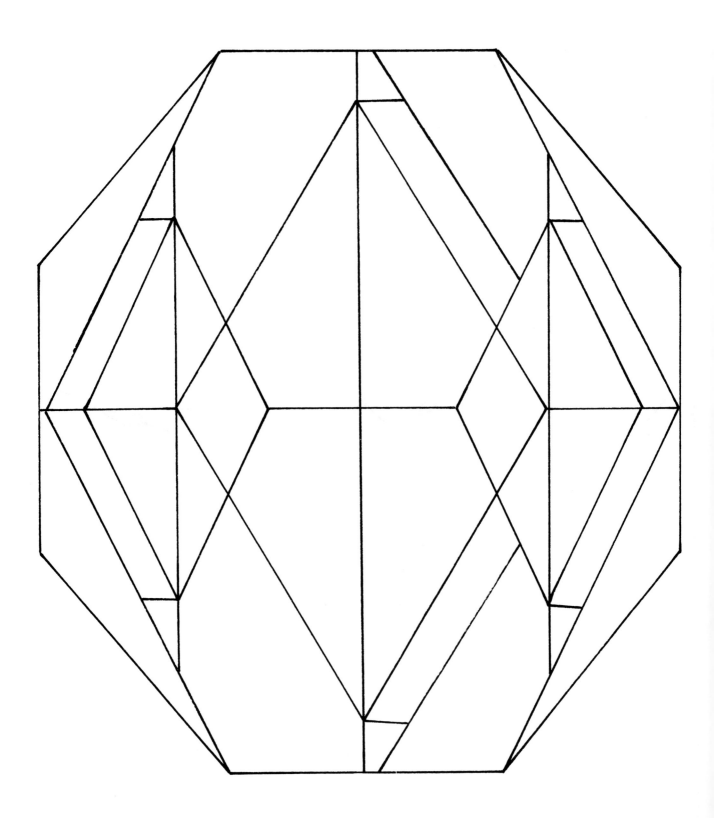

12 DESIGNS BEHIND THE PHOTOGRAPHS

Drawings for the sculptures on pages 17, 18 and 27 are not provided

page 40

page 28

page 28

page 29

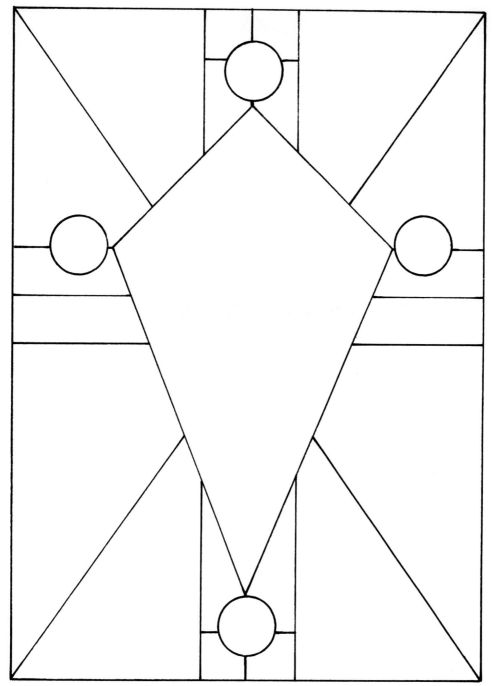

page 30

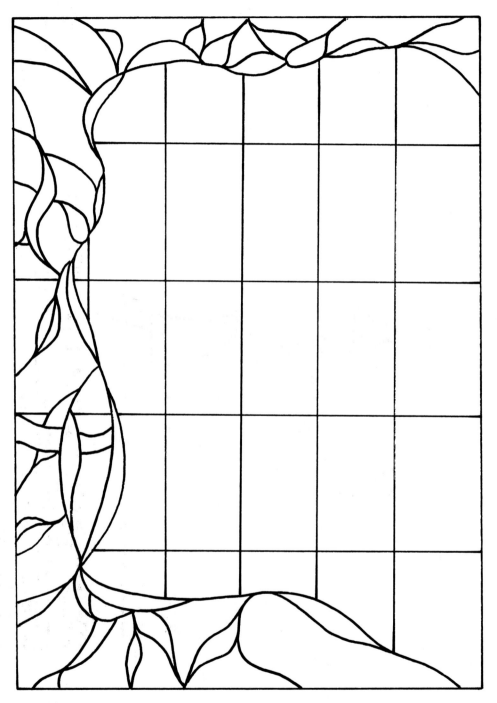

page 39

opposite: page 39

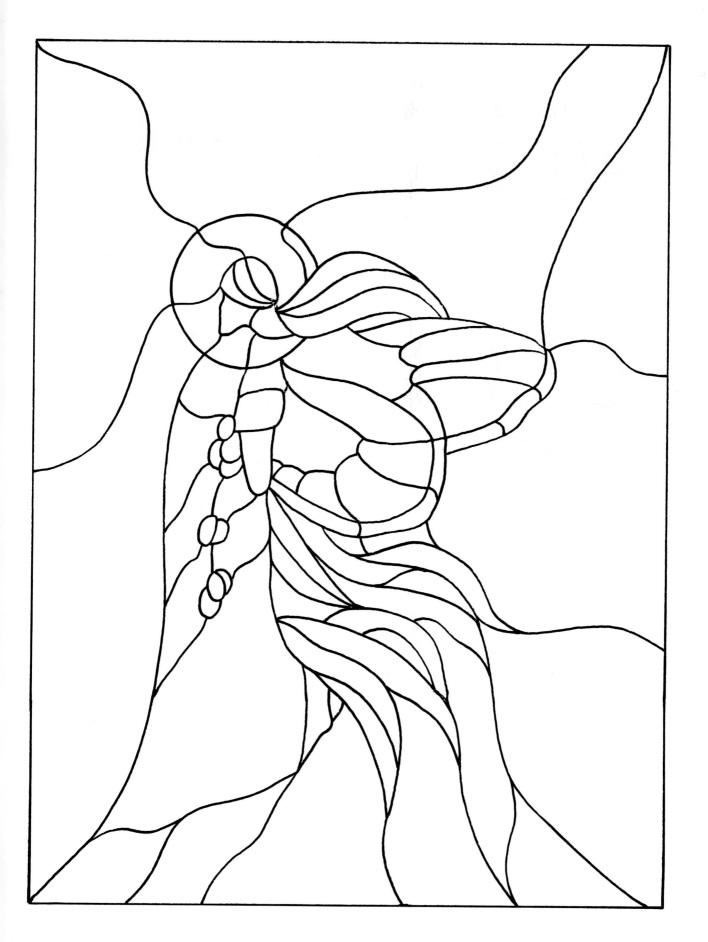

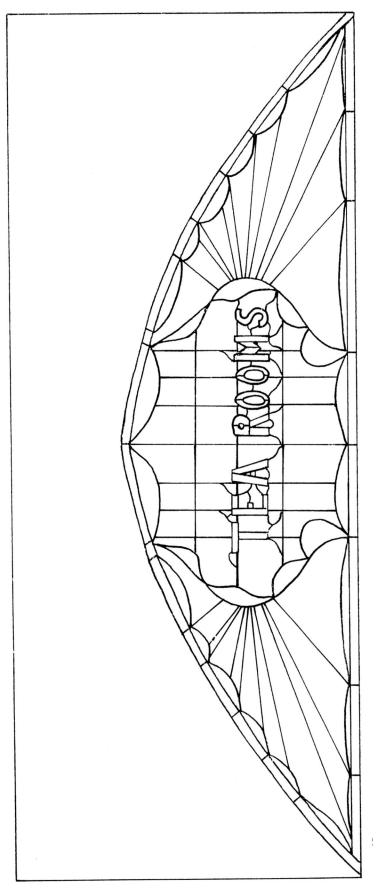

page 40

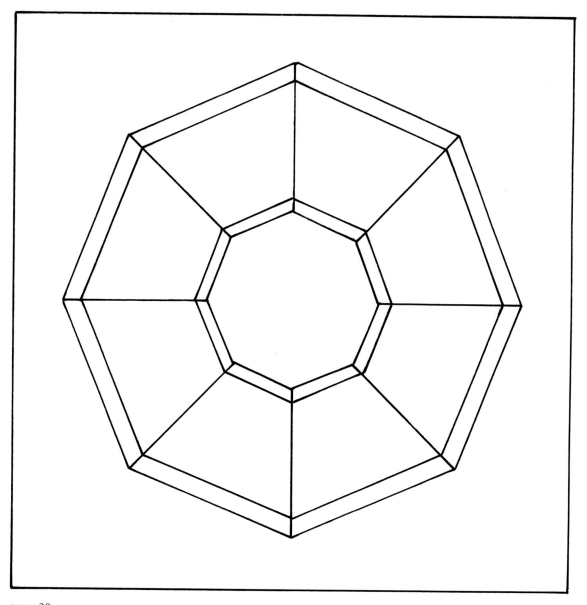

page 30

POSTSCRIPT

Most State and local government-funded Small Business Centres and work schemes for the unemployed now recognise the validity of individuals pursuing creative business occupations such as leadlighting.

Business training schemes available through these Centres provide courses which are invaluable in providing the novice with a sound grounding in the ways of commerce.

It would be well worth your while to investigate the schemes operating in your area.

INDEX